CONTEMPLATIVE PRAYER
A Guide for Today's Catholic

REVISED AND EXPANDED

*Featuring an
8-Day Personal Retreat*

Jim Borst, M.H.M.

**ONE LIGUORI DRIVE
LIGUORI, MO 63057-9999
(314) 464-2500**

Imprimi Potest:
James Shea, C.SS.R.
Provincial, St. Louis Province
The Redemptorists

Imprimatur:
Monsignor Maurice F. Byrne
Vice Chancellor, Archdiocese of St. Louis

ISBN 0-89243-522-4
Library of Congress Catalog Card Number: 92-75939

Originally published by ASIAN TRADING CORPORATION, P.O. Box 11029, Bombay—400 020.

Cover design by Chris Sharp

TABLE OF CONTENTS

PREFACE TO THE
REVISED AND EXPANDED
EDITION

In 1972 Father Henri Le Saux, a French Benedictine who had come to India in 1947 to live out his Benedictine vocation as an Indian sannyasi, urged me to publish some notes I had written on a method of contemplative prayer. During his life Father Le Saux did much to call us back to a contemplative experience of God. It was his wish that these notes be made available in a handy format to individual religious, priests, and laity who are eager to set out on the road where they could meet the risen Lord.

That first published edition had eleven printings in India, with a dozen editions and translations abroad, among them *Contemplative Prayer: A Guide for Today's Catholic,* published by Liguori Publications in 1979.

Now I present a revised and expanded edition. The "method" is the same, but I have added several "phases" (Longing Love, Forgiving From the Heart, Asking in Faith); a schedule for an eight-day self-directed retreat; and some fresh insights into contemplative prayer. The material has also been rearranged somewhat. It is my sincere hope that this revised and expanded edition will prove to be a useful handbook for all who love God and want to know him more.

Deciding to pray is the first essential step: a decision to give to God an hour of daily time faithfully, regardless of the cost. In giving our time, we give ourselves; in surrender and expectation, we open ourselves to his presence.

It is clear that obstacles, at times recurring obstacles, need to be removed, as they bind our inner selves and burden our heart. There will often be the need for a deeper surrender of cares and worry, for acceptance of his loving presence in every circumstance, for repentance and true forgiveness. Distractions of the heart that cannot be bypassed need to be worked through in prayer before a totally free heart can stretch out its longings toward him.

It is also clear that if we want to give God the first priority in our life, we have to resist the temptation to fill our mind with TV, movies, and other modern distractions and adopt a disciplined, God-oriented lifestyle. "Blessed are the poor in spirit and the clean of heart. They shall see God."

He calls us: " 'Come.' Let the one who thirsts come forward, and the one who wants it receive the gift of life-giving water" (Revelation 22:17).

Father Jim Borst, M.H.M.
Baramulla, Kashmir
India
August 5, 1991

FOREWORD

Contemplative Prayer—please don't let that title put you off. This excellent little booklet is a popular discussion of prayer in its quiet, reflective mode.

Father Jim Borst, the author, lives in India. He is deeply involved in active ministry there, with a special concern for youth. He knows what it means not to have time to pray, which is an excuse many of us use for not praying as much as we should. But as they used to say in the military service, that's an explanation, not an excuse. We *can* find time for quiet prayer if we really consider it sufficiently important. Father Borst convincingly argues the case for its importance.

In case the news hasn't reached you, there has been a remarkable resurgence of interest in contemplative prayer in the past two or three decades. Publishers vie with one another in getting titles on this subject for their catalogs and bookstores. Henri Nouwen, Thomas Keating, Basil Pennington, Carlo Carretto, William Johnston, George Maloney, Edward Farrell, to name a few, are gifted and prolific writers, and their books are eagerly awaited by a substantial reading audience.

And now there is this booklet, modest in size, answering in an unpretentious and readable way the basic questions: *What is contemplative prayer? Why should I make use of it? How can I best practice it?*

Not too many years ago, contemplative prayer was generally regarded as an exotic growth in the Church, reserved for a small group of eccentrics who opted to immure themselves behind gray walls of convents and monasteries. There they lived out their lives in silence, completely apart from the affairs of the world.

The one man chiefly responsible for changing that image was Thomas Merton. A convert to the Catholic faith, Merton entered the Trappist abbey at Gethsemani, Kentucky, in 1941 at age twenty-six. His autobiography, *The Seven Storey Mountain,* published in 1948, quickly became one of the most widely read books, not only in the United States but throughout the world. In the years before his tragic death, Thomas Merton published forty major volumes. Exploring every aspect of contemplative prayer, Merton's books had a powerful impact on the generation that came to maturity in the fifties and sixties.

On December 10, 1968, Merton died in Bangkok, Thailand, electrocuted by faulty wiring in an electrical appliance. At the time, he was scheduled to be one of the leading speakers at an international conference of spiritual leaders from Eastern and Western spiritual traditions who had gathered to discuss modes of contemplative prayer.

It was Merton's firm belief that the most pressing need in the contemporary world for people in all walks of life is to understand and to practice reflective prayer. Only in this way, he wrote, can we deepen our self-understanding and capacity to love. Without that deepening process, even though we are well-intentioned, we will not have anything of value to give to others or to the world.

In 1963, while Merton was busy writing and training novices in his monastery, the encyclical *Pacem in Terris* appeared. In it, Pope John XXIII described what he termed the "three distinctive characteristics of our age."

1. He saw working people as extending with increasing clamor their claim to equality on the socio-economic and political levels.
2. He recognized a phenomenon we have grown familiar with: that women would demand an increasingly active role in all areas of public concern.
3. He saw the Third World nations as exerting increasing pressure on the rest of the world to grant them equal status and a fair share of this world's goods.

How prophetic this aging pontiff was! In 1963 the developments he pointed to were in their infancy, but they have grown steadily in their significance and impact over the past thirty years.

What, you may be asking, has all this to do with contemplative prayer?

A brief passage in *Pacem in Terris* reveals the contemplative orientation of its author. This passage may be taken as another sign Pope John thought must be fulfilled before the peace he dreamed of could be realized:

Every believer in this world of ours must be a spark of light, a center of love, a vivifying leaven amidst his fellow men. But he will be this all the more perfectly, the more closely he lives in communion with God in the intimacy of his own soul.

Pope John XXIII, the social reformer, and Thomas Merton, the contemplative, are not all that far apart. We cannot have lasting social reform unless we bring a genuine contemplative spirit to the world. And we cannot be genuine contemplatives unless we are conscious of and distressed by the ills and problems of the human family.

There are two basic needs in the human heart that contemplative prayer serves. Father Borst expresses them in two separate sections of this booklet. First, contemplative prayer helps us discover our true self. Second, contemplative prayer cultivates community life.

Each of us has a need to speak to God out of the uniqueness that is God's special gift to us. "When you pray," Christ said, "go to your inner room, close the door, and pray to your Father in secret. And your Father who sees in secret will repay you" (Matthew 6:6). These words are a warning about ostentation in the prayer practices of the Pharisees. But there is a meaning beyond that, illustrated by Jesus' own practice. As the gospels mention a dozen times or more, Jesus would go out into the desert or to a mountaintop to be alone and to commune with his Father in solitary prayer.

Every one of us *needs* that kind of desert or mountaintop experience at regular intervals. Otherwise, we glide along on the surface of life, empty and bored, no matter how busy we are in external affairs. Without that experience, our potential for genuine growth in love and understanding remains unrealized.

There is another need that must also be served, however: the need for strength and support from our community and our corresponding duty to contribute to the welfare of the community. As Charles Peguy expressed it: "One Christian is no Christian." He also wrote: "When we get to heaven, God is going to ask us first, 'Where are the others?' "

But by a proven paradox, it is in the secret room of prayer that love and concern for these "others" begin to grow, like flowers in a hothouse.

Those who read this booklet attentively will sense, I feel sure, that even in his busy life as a missionary the author has found a way of living "in communion with God in the intimacy of his soul."

Father Borst could not have written this quietly earnest and important little booklet if that were not the case.

Louis G. Miller, C.SS.R.

I.
WHAT IS
CONTEMPLATIVE PRAYER?

The Three Stages of Prayer

Before attempting to describe contemplative prayer, we will do well first to take a look at the three classical stages of prayer.

- VOCAL PRAYER is a prayer of the lips, with stress on words, recited or sung. The text of vocal prayer may be readymade, such as the Our Father or the Twenty-third Psalm, and is often beautiful and inspiring. Vocal prayer may also be a spontaneous pouring out to God in our own words of what is in our heart.
- MEDITATIVE PRAYER, or meditation, is prayer centered in the mind, which forms pictures and ponders them and reflects on God and his wonderful

dealings. The mind seeks understanding and insight. In meditation, the lips are quiet and the mind is active.

- CONTEMPLATIVE PRAYER, or contemplation, is prayer of the heart and will that reaches out to God's presence. The lips and the mind both come to rest. There is a simple gazing at the Lord, while the heart reaches out in wordless prayer and the will seeks to be one with the will of God.

The Two Stages of Contemplative Prayer

Contemplative prayer is usually divided into two further stages:

- ACQUIRED CONTEMPLATION, when, with faith, hope, and a longing love, we reach out to God's presence. It begins from a knowing in faith that he is really present and a seeking with all our heart to touch him and to be touched by him.
- INFUSED CONTEMPLATION, when, through God's grace, as a free gift, he gives us a real awareness of his presence, for example, through experiencing the fruits of the Holy Spirit—love, joy, peace, and so forth; through an awareness of his presence in our heart; or in other ways.

I used to wonder whether infused contemplation was only for some gifted individuals or for everyone. I found the answer in the words of Jesus: "And I tell you, ask and you will receive; seek and you will find; knock and the door will be opened to you" (Luke 11:9). With this promise, I felt that contemplation was also for me. "The LORD's love for us is strong; / the LORD is faithful forever" (Psalm 117:2).

The Prayer of the Heart

How many hearts do we have? Most of us think first of the *physical heart,* a vital organ necessary for the circulation of the blood situated left of center in the chest. But each human being also has a *spiritual heart,* the center of self-identity and of the spiritual dimension of our being. We spontaneously point to this spiritual heart at the center of our chest when we refer to ourselves as *me* and when we speak of the "core of my being," "the bottom of my heart," "my deepest self." We refer to it when we pray "Come into my heart, Lord Jesus" and when we receive the risen Lord as the Bread of Life in the holy Eucharist: "He dwells in me (in my heart), and I dwell in him (in his heart)." Most pictures of the Sacred Heart of Jesus position his heart at the center of his chest to symbolize his spiritual heart, his inner being, his inner self.

Most of us are only vaguely aware of our spiritual heart, however. We may experience it only as a center of emotions: love, joy, sorrow, anger, peace, fear, loneliness, pain. But this heart has deeper layers of self-awareness that can be opened to others, especially to the Lord. Our spiritual heart can expand to embrace everyone, the whole world. Our heart has been created to become his dwelling place. In the deepest depth of our heart is the image and likeness of God, our true identity as his true sons and daughters. Here he dwells by grace as the source of the spring of living water, as the source of true love, flowing through our heart.

Mature Christians are meant to reach the stage of contemplative prayer. We can compare the three stages of prayer to levels of schooling. We begin in the primary grades with reading and writing—vocal prayer. The middle grades of prayer consist of meditation, where reflection on life and revelation is the main subject, although vocal prayer is not neglected. The high school of prayer is the beginning of contemplative prayer such as is recommended here. We do not forget or neglect what we have learned at the lower levels, but the growing point of our prayer life is an awakening to God's presence and an opening to his Spirit.

In comparing contemplative prayer to vocal prayer, we could say that in contemplative prayer we seek an awareness that what is contained in the words we say in vocal prayer is really and truly present to us. In using the words "Our Father who art in heaven," we go beyond the words to an awareness of God's presence deep within us, and we dwell in that presence. The actual words used are like the ringing of a bell that awakens us from sleep to consciousness of God's presence within.

If we compare contemplative prayer to meditative prayer, we could say that instead of mulling over the truth reflectively, we come to a halt and gaze at it, awakening to God's presence within. Meditation could be compared to the activity that goes into making and painting a picture. Contemplative prayer is the quiet looking at the completed picture, seeing it as a whole, becoming aware of the reality of the artist's vision it portrays.

Beyond words, thoughts, and concepts, we seek to enter a

reality that is spiritual and true, enduring and overpowering: God himself the Father, Jesus his beloved Son, and their Spirit. The mind cannot see or grasp this reality, but love can discern it. The Spirit awakens this love and surrender. The author of *The Cloud of Unknowing* (written about 1350 by an unknown author) says, therefore, "Though we cannot know him we can love him. By love he may be touched and embraced, never by thought." The Lord may graciously return this love, and so Saint John of the Cross can say, "Contemplation is nothing else but a secret, peaceful infusion of God, which, if admitted, will set the soul on fire with the Spirit of love."

Contemplative prayer is the only *real* prayer in the sense that it leads beyond words (vocal prayer) and thoughts (meditative prayer) to the reality toward which words and thought point. In this sense, *all* prayer must have a *real* or *contemplative quality* because vocal prayer may never be just a recitation of words, and meditative prayer may never be just an exercise in thinking.

Pentecostal Prayer

In contemplative prayer we seek the reality of our own spirit and of the Spirit of God. This prayer opens us to the action and gifts of the Holy Spirit. It also opens our spirit unreservedly to the cleansing and healing of the Holy Spirit in an awareness of his presence.

Contemplative prayer may be called pentecostal prayer in the sense that through it we seek an awareness of the indwelling Spirit, given by Jesus as our comforter. Jesus, in John 14:16, promised that the Advocate would be with us always and would supply us with all the spiritual gifts we need.

We must begin our pilgrimage to the mountain of the Lord on our own two feet. There are maps and guides, and we must not fail to ask people we meet on the way. But we must also remember that it is the breath of the Spirit that carries us forward and upward. It is the glory of the Lord dimly seen at the end that draws us onward. And we must not forget to consult the guidebooks at times.

Other Names for Contemplation

Saint Teresa of Avila called contemplation the prayer of *recollection.* The following are other ways various spiritual writers have described contemplative prayer:

- prayer of simplicity
- prayer of silence
- prayer of repose
- prayer of the simple presence of God
- prayer of loving attention
- prayer of the heart

Background of Contemplative Prayer

Priests and religious are frequently asked, "What form of prayer do you use?" People see our lifelong dedication to the service of mankind; they recognize in our celibacy a discipline disposing us to prayer; they surmise the secret of our strength to be a prayerful union with God, the full realization of his presence within us; and they are eager to know how we have arrived at this.

Yet the ordinary priest or religious finds the question hard to deal with. We are not accustomed to reflect on the ways, means, and objectives of prayer and what it demands of the one who prays. Most of us have learned the practice of prayer by reciting certain prescribed prayers, such as the Divine Office, the Mass prayers, and the rosary; by making half an hour's meditation; and by occasional direct *private* prayer to God.

We often feel that provided we are faithful to our prayer routine, we have done our duty. In fact, the main objectives of teaching prayer in the seminaries and novitiates seem to have been to initiate people into the prayer program expected of priests and religious and to inculcate a sense of faithful observance of this program.

The program included a simple form of meditation or mental prayer, practiced as part of the daily schedule. Such daily practice would help us along the path of prayer through life. Contemplative prayer, which is beyond prayerful reflection and exercises of the imagination and will, was hardly ever pointed out as a natural development of prayer life. The impression most often conveyed was that it was beyond the reach and proper ambition of ordinary priests, religious, and laity.

There are several historical reasons why the Church shied away from an emphasis on contemplative prayer during the last few centuries. Indeed, not only did Christians fail to appreciate such prayer, it was viewed with actual suspicion for centuries.

This view was partially due to the excesses of late medieval extremists, such as the illuminists of Spain, whose view was derived from a misinterpretation of infused contemplation, and the Quietest controversy of seventeenth-century France. Quietism, in the words of Father Thomas Keating, "consisted in making once and for all an act of love for God by which you gave yourself entirely to him with the intention never to recall the surrender. As long as you never withdrew the intention to belong to God, divine union was assured. No further need for effort, either in prayer or outside it, was required."

Contemplative prayer, however, unlike the above description, demands ongoing effort. True, the emotions, the mind, and the imagination are quietened in this kind of prayer, but the heart and the will are focused on the Lord. This is the "longing love" described in *The Cloud of Unknowing*.

As a result of the controversy, an irrational horror of Quietism prevailed for some time, and no one dared even breathe the name of "contemplation." A consequent lack of true perspective in the religious life and in the lives of many priests committed to celibacy was the result. This was disastrous because religious vows express a dedication to the Lord and his kingdom that predisposes and leads toward knowledge in love of God, experienced in faith. When the cornerstone of contemplative prayer is no longer explicitly present in the fabric of religious life, a lack of orientation and a distortion of perspective follow. Love of God, the primary commandment, must always have first place. In a similar way, celibacy only makes sense at a personal level if it includes a sharing in the knowledge and love of God.

Despite these difficulties, however, genuine contemplative prayer survived and actually flourished in the Church and in the lives of saints and devoted Christians. In our own day, it seems the Lord wants to restore this remarkable gift to the whole of God's people.

One spiritual writer declared the practice of contemplative prayer in silence and solitude, preferably before the Lord in the Blessed Sacrament, to be the most meaningful part of the life of priests and religious. An experience of contemplative prayer has been recommended as a necessary preparation for those wishing to be ordained to the diocesan priesthood and for missionaries. Vatican Council II also urged all religious to combine the apostolate with contemplation: "[They] ought to seek God before all else, and solely; they should join contemplation, by which they cleave to God by mind and heart, to apostolic love" (*Decree on Religious Life,* 5).

Truly, the Spirit of God seems to be breathing over our spiritually starved and secularized society and is bringing it to new life, especially through an awakening of young people.

Many people in the West have taken up Asian forms of prayer such as Buddhist meditation, Zen, transcendental meditation, and Yoga prayer. While these Eastern forms are contemplative in character, those using them may lack the spiritual guidance of God's revealed Word. They may focus on other names than "Father," "Son," and "Holy Spirit," and they may pursue other goals than union-in-love with God. However, many sincerely seek identity in a self-indulgent and materialist society through these prayer forms.

In India, true contemplative prayer is an answer to a widespread and deep longing for "God-realization." Indians often ask us, "Have you found God? Have you realized God?" In contemplative prayer we reach out to God with a longing love, until he gives us his grace and his presence in our heart, and we allow him to grow in us and to fill our whole being.

Relationship to Charismatic Prayer

As already mentioned, in silent prayer, as in a charismatic prayer group, there is a movement toward complete surrender to the Spirit of God in love, peace, joy, and thanksgiving. For this reason, contemplation is closely connected to the Charismatic Renewal Movement. In both these forms of contemplative prayer, there is also the opening of heart and life to the gifts and fruits of the Spirit of Jesus, who leads us to the Father.

It appears likely that in the coming years a new outpouring of the Spirit among God's people and a reintegration of true contemplative prayer into the life of the Church will form the heart of a lasting renewal. This may well be the answer to the prayer of Pope John XXIII, who, in convoking the Second Vatican Council, addressed these words to the Holy Spirit: "Renew thy wonderful works in this age of ours through a new Pentecost, as it were, and grant to the Holy Church that, persevering in ardent prayer in union with Mary the Mother of Jesus and under the leadership of the Blessed Peter, she may spread the kingdom of the divine Savior, the kingdom of truth and justice, the kingdom of love and of peace. Amen."

II.

WHY PRACTICE
CONTEMPLATIVE PRAYER?

We might sometimes get the impression that contemplative prayer does not belong to the gospel of Christ, that it is at best a discipline taken by the Church from non-Christian religions and adapted to the Christian life. Of course, many people outside the Christian tradition eagerly seek and find God in prayer. A careful study of the gospels and of the Christian traditions, however, reveals that contemplative prayer is at the heart of the gospel and of the Christian life. It was the prayer of the prophets and the humble of the Old Testament, of those who—seeking the face of the Lord—endeavored to love the Lord their God with all their heart, with all their soul, and with all their strength (Deuteronomy 6:5) and to worship him in the contemplative peace and rest of the Sabbath.

Contemplative prayer is also the prayer of Jesus, of Mary, and of the saints. A study of the lives of almost all holy people will bring this prayer to light as the heart of their discipleship and their Christian lives.

It Is the Prayer of Jesus

Jesus experienced his oneness with God also in and through his human nature, which is in every way like our own except for sin. "Therefore, he had to become like his brothers in every way, that he might be a merciful and faithful high priest before God to expiate the sins of the people" (Hebrews 2:17).

We see how Jesus sought to live a life of solitude, privacy, silence, fasting, and watching in prayer—conditions that render human nature more open to the Spirit, make it a better instrument of prayer, and provide a better atmosphere for union in knowledge and love with the Father. It was in such silent prayer that Jesus learned to know his Father's will and experience complete surrender in love. In prayer he heard the word his Father speaks (John 17:8, 14), and in prayer he knew his Father in love (John 10:15 and Matthew 11:25-27).

By sharing his Spirit of love and surrender with his disciples, he gave them a share in his union with his Father (John 17:20-21). In this way we have become adopted sons and daughters, sharing by grace what Jesus, our Brother, is in his very being. "...if children, then heirs, heirs of God and joint heirs with Christ, if only we suffer with him so that we may also be glorified with him" (Romans 8:17).

Jesus, then, wants us to share in his own experience (in his human nature) of kinship of the Father in the love of the Spirit (Romans 8:28-30). In contemplative prayer we are led to recreate the prayer experience of our Lord, though in a very imperfect and faltering manner, to be made complete in the light of his glory (1 Corinthians 13:12 and 1 John 3:2).

It Is the Prayer of Mary

A significant clue to the understanding of Mary's spiritual life is her strange decision not to marry, a decision made before the Annunciation (Luke 1:31-34) in the face of Jewish tradition and of public opinion against the unmarried state. This decision points to the unique grace that filled Mary from the beginning. At a very early age, she must have opened herself to an awareness of God and experienced the joy of living before his face, the joy of being blessed with his smile (Numbers 6:25). Instinctively, she shied away from sin and evil as casting a shadow over her and tending to close her person to the Lord.

In Mary's heart lived the grace of the *anawim,* the humble of heart, the poor of the Lord who single-mindedly seek his face and praise his name and whose spirituality is so admirably expressed in Psalm 34:4-23:

> Magnify the LORD with me;
>   let us exalt his name together.
> I sought the LORD, who answered me...
> Look to God that you may be radiant with joy...
> Learn to savor how good the LORD is...
>   seek peace and pursue it....
>   no one is condemned whose refuge is God.

Instinctively, she was drawn to a way of life that would keep her free for the Lord, not merely in outward service but in inward service of praise and thanksgiving. She saw herself as the Lord's handmaid, single-mindedly attentive to his presence. If the Lord was going to bring salvation to his people through a poor and humble servant of the Lord (Isaiah 42, 49, 50, 52), then she would be a poor and humble servant of the Lord, expressing in her whole of life a bridal love and faithfulness that Israel as a people so conspicuously lacked.

Thus she felt drawn to a decision, if not to a vow, not to marry—a decision involving complete surrender in faith to his guidance. So the Lord led her to a young man named Joseph, who was gifted with a similar grace.

She was a thoughtful person (Luke 2:19), treasuring in her heart the traditional poetic prayer songs (Psalms) and reflecting on the Lord's messages through the prophets. She had the contemplative's feelings for language and when inspired would express her own prayer in traditional song. (See Luke 1:46-55).

She must have initiated Jesus into the Jewish ways of prayer. As the mother of Jesus, his teacher of prayer, and an aunt of the hermitlike prophet John the Baptist, Mary must have spent much time quietly in prayer and contemplation. In the last mention of her in Scripture, we find her in continuous prayer with the disciples, pleading for the outpouring of the Spirit her Son had promised. (See Acts of the Apostles 1:14.)

We may surely think of Mary as the "Contemplative Rose" or the "Mystical Rose," as the "Rose of Sharon," "A Tower of Ivory," or the "Morning Star," symbolizing the beauty of a woman deeply loved and deeply in love, longing for God's presence and for union with him, spreading fragrance with the freshness of spring.

Other Reasons to Practice Contemplative Prayer

It promotes relaxation in God's presence.

Contemplative prayer involves a search for peace, tranquillity, and serenity. We seek to meet the Lord of the Sabbath in his place of rest deep within us and during an hour of rest and relaxation in his presence give him the worship of our life.

A major task, therefore, during this hour is to release tension, calm down, surrender to him in faith so that at his word the storm may cease, and accept his will. "Seek peace and pursue it" (Psalm 34:15), not with a violent effort but with a gentle letting go of all tension, excitement, anxiety, worry, desire, hatred, and self-pity.

Concentration is a word often heard in connection with contemplative prayer. Perhaps a better word is *attention*. But this should not evolve from a mighty and tense effort. What is called for here is a gentle letting go of things, a relaxing of undue concern about people and situations, and a release from worry and anxiety.

While all these gently flow out of us, there remains only one thing: attention to the Lord, awareness of the presence of him who is the Author and Giver of all peace and strength.

It fosters nonviolence of heart and mind.

A firm commitment to live a peaceful life is both a condition for and a fruit of contemplative prayer. Our peace may be disturbed by all seven capital sins, those vicious tendencies that can hold us in their grip: pride, jealousy, anger, gluttony, lust, laziness, and greed.

Among these, the main disturber of our peace will probably be the passion of anger. This at least has been suggested by Evagrius Ponticus, a mystical theologian who lived in the last half of the fourth century. Any yielding to anger (which includes rancor, suspicion, antipathy, bitterness, peevishness, touchiness) is bound to be paid for at the time of prayer. Prayer is a useful barometer, indicating unabashedly our times of calm and of storm. "Prayer is the off shoot of gentleness and the absence of anger" (Evagrius). At the root of anger lies a desire for and an attachment to worldly things and values. This is why Evagrius asks: "What in fact would a man have to get angry about if he cared nothing for food, wealth, human prestige, and so on?"

In contemplative prayer we must be wholeheartedly committed to the mind of Jesus as testified by his indwelling Spirit, as revealed in the gospels, and as proclaimed in the Sermon on the Mount. This means no violence, no hatred, no evil desire, no revenge, no judging; it means gentleness, compassion, willingness to give and to share, an outgoing love and forgiveness for those who harm you.

I have also found a sober and simple lifestyle necessary to keep the heart and the mind free for this prayer. If we keep our heart and mind free for God, we can certainly enjoy the good gifts of reading or TV watching occasionally, but true contemplative prayer is incompatible with escapist habits that overload the mind and bind the heart.

It improves the quality of life.

My experience is that the fruits and benefits of a daily discipline of contemplative prayer are given not so much during the time of prayer but rather outside it. The prayer affects the quality of life.

During the time of prayer, we may often have a sense of wasting our time, of mental distraction, of sleepiness. Yet the seeking of our heart and our will for God and the graceful effects of his Real Presence ground us deeper in him.

Outside our time of prayer, however poor, we find that we remember his presence spontaneously from time to time. It may be a moment when we thank him or when we tell him "I love you." Also, there is a deeper peace in us; we can work better and cope better with people and things. We are more eager to serve him and to do only what he asks of us. What counts is not what pleases us but what he asks of us.

In the long run, this daily prayer has a transforming effect on our whole life.

It transforms the personality.

Slowly but surely, contemplative prayer will lead to a wonderful transformation of the personality. Clearly, our spirituality and our prayer must be effective in changing us, or it will be pointless and disgraceful. We cannot *pray* day after day, month after month, and remain the same. If we do not change, our prayer is not genuine prayer but a subtle way of hiding ourselves from the living God, a subtle way of keeping the Spirit from intruding into our life. Real contemplative prayer involves an opening to the Spirit. The gifts and fruits of the Spirit (Galatians 5:22) will be further evidence. Through contemplative prayer, we experience more fully Jesus' personal gift to everyone—his peace (John 14:27). We are healed daily in the living water of his Spirit, and we continue to advance toward full maturity in Christ.

The author of the *Cloud* describes this transformation in a delightful manner:

As a person matures in the work of love, he will discover that this love governs his demeanor befittingly both within and without. When grace draws a man to contemplation it seems to transfigure him even physically so that though he may be ill-favored by nature, he now appears changed and lovely to behold. His whole personality becomes so attractive that good people are honored and delighted to be in his company, strengthened by the sense of God he radiates.

And so, do your part to co-operate with grace and win this great gift, for truly it will teach the man who possesses it how to govern himself and all that is his. He will even be able to discern the character and temperament of others when necessary. He will know how to accommodate himself to everyone, and (to the astonishment of all) even to inveterate sinners, without sinning himself. God's grace will work through him, drawing others to desire that very contemplative love which the

Spirit awakens in him. His countenance and conversation will be rich in spiritual wisdom, fire, and the fruits of love, for he will speak with a calm assurance devoid of falsehood and the fawning pretense of hypocrites.

The author goes on to paint a painfully true picture of persons who pretend to this transformation but who do not pray.

His point surely is that those who have learned to be relaxed, outgoing, and at ease with God are the same with other people; and that whereas nervous and irritable (*angry*) people are most unpleasant company, we love to meet a person who radiates peace and strength, whose sympathy is positive and outgoing, and who is aware, moreover, of *our* "character and temperament."

Saint John of the Cross taught that a deep life of prayer in the Spirit comes more quickly to those who are given to solitary prayer. And Saint Teresa of Avila wrote that if we will try to live in the presence of God for one year, we will see ourselves at the end of that year at the height of perfection without knowing it.

In our own time, a witness who prefers to remain unidentified gives this modest yet equally positive testimony:

After less than two years serious effort in contemplative prayer, I recognize the following changes have taken place within me:

Joy, peace, calm, now reign where before there was fear, tension, unrest of all kinds. Even in difficult situations and decisions, peace remains and solutions are brought about in most unexpected ways—not products of my own wisdom, for they just seem to happen without my knowing how.

Growing convictions of the reality that is God and of his Spirit, glimpses of the Fatherhood of God, a sense of personal dignity and worth because of his personal love for me have replaced former self-hatred and negativism.

Acceptance of my work (its unpleasant duties), of criticism in peace and a more loving surrender; more tolerance and acceptance of others, with less irritability—these are now mine. Given my proud temperament and nature, I see that—through God's mercy—I have been prevented from many tragedies. Through a gradual discovery of my false humility, I now have a real desire for truth. Many psychological ills have come to light, making me more free.

There is a greater appreciation of the gift of vocation and more stability and genuineness in striving to live it. Other prayers and devotions are more meaningful. Desire for God has grown. This gives me more courage in the striving; whereas formerly I was much given to despondency and self-pity.

I think it is true that faith, hope, and love have been deepened. I long to share this treasure.

It helps us discover our true self.

Another wholesome effect of this prayer is that through the action of the Holy Spirit we become more fully and more truly human.

Before God, in his presence, we learn the necessity of being absolutely true to ourselves. We learn to see ourselves as we truly are behind the mask of conventions, behind our poses and pretensions, behind our little and big deceptions. Gradually outgrowing artificiality in thought, word, and deed; false attitudes; and our false self; we grow in truthfulness and genuineness. We become more truly ourselves the more we live in God's presence.

As we become more true to ourselves, because more true to God, we will also be more true to our surroundings (that is, more objective in our search for knowledge and in our evaluation of information) and more true to the people we live with. Our capacity for genuine interpersonal relationship will increase. True charity—the ability to enter sympathetically into other people's feelings, situations, needs—goes with true prayer, which is the ability to be open and true to God and to ourselves. How true the words of Saint John: He who says that he knows God and hates his brother is a liar!

Sebastian Temple expresses something similar in his song of the Happy Man:

Happy the man who wanders with the Lord,
Happy the man who knows how to live,
Happy the man who never seeks reward,
Giving because he loves to give.

He seeks no gold,
He wants no gain,
He knows those things are all in vain.
He needs no praise nor honor too,
His only motto: "To your own self be true."

Happy the man who learned how to pray,
Happy the man who has a burning goal,
Happy the man whose service needs no pay,
This man has found his own soul.
Happy the man,
Happy the man of the Lord.

It strengthens our prayer life.

Contemplative prayer brings a new meaning and sense of unity to our other prayers. We move away from a routine way of praying that follows a prescribed program. We feel the need and gradually obtain the ability to give all prayers a contemplative quality, making them into real prayer rather than merely reciting them or saying them in a singsong way.

Initially, it may well be that we feel the need for a reduction of set vocal prayers and avoidance of repetition; we feel an inability to accept as normal any prayer that is hurried or said slovenly without due reverence or regard to its sense. Later on, however, we may well be moved to return to more vocal prayer, especially of the repetitive kind (private rosary, instant prayers, the Jesus Prayer, and so on) because it helps us dwell in the presence of God and to "wander with him."

In his "Norms for Implementing the Decree: On the Up-to-Date Renewal of Religious Life" (August 6, 1966), Pope Paul VI highly commended the practice of mental prayer:

In order that religious may share more intimately and with greater profit in the holy mystery of the Eucharist, and in the public prayer of the Church, and that their interior life be more abundantly nourished, priority should be given to mental prayer over a multiplicity of other prayers. However, those community exercises which are traditional in the Church should be preserved and care taken that religious be rightly instructed in the ways of the religious life (21).

The Church has carried out this norm by shortening and simplifying the prayers of the Divine Office and the Mass. By doing so, it has made them into real and meaningful prayers and at the same time provided more time for personal contemplative prayer.

It cultivates community life.

Most of us have a number of irritating, habitual faults and weaknesses that we cannot overcome in spite of good intentions—criticism, impatience, loss of temper, harsh words, grudges, moods of depression. These faults disrupt our peace with others, with ourselves, and with God. A sincere effort to seek God in silence and surrender through contemplative prayer will gradually lessen the impact of such faults and reduce them. A person who contemplates and continues to strive for sanctity dries up the root of sin that remains even after confession.

Contemplative prayer will help to greatly reduce the tension resulting from habitual faults, especially as it affects people living in community, where there is constant need of being available and open to others.

The practice of this prayer will be more helpful toward

building up a genuine community life than perhaps frequent dialogue (which, too, has an essential role to play). In dialogue, there is a tendency to stress the importance of the issue. In silent prayer, the seeking of love and peace is *the* issue to which all other issues are subordinated; and even when a painful decision has to be made, we are led to proceed without violence.

Everyone needs a daily rhythm of sleep and wakefulness, of work and relaxation, of eating food and digesting it. It seems that a daily hour for the "healing of the soul," for a coming to rest in a movement of love, is a practical necessity for living a balanced human and Christian life—whether in community or not.

In this connection, Douglas V. Steere makes the following comment: "When a Hindu lives in an American home for a month and asks his host when is the time in the day that he takes for the healing of the soul, this is ecumenical crossfire that is not easily shaken off." There are priests and religious who formerly prayed a great deal—at the time when their vocation became clear to them or at the seminary or novitiate—but their daily routine of duties and spiritual exercises has now crowded out sustained personal prayer. They will welcome this opportunity to return to more intensive personal prayer, making it the center of their vocation and their lives.

The challenge of contemplation can and should be accepted by all—priests, religious, and laity—as a personal covenant with the Lord. The daily hour of prayer is the outward sign of this covenant, in which we surrender ourselves to the Lord and the Lord gives himself to us. This covenant is the full-grown fruit of our baptismal commitment, and it is ever celebrated and renewed in the Eucharist of the New Covenant of the Lord and his people.

III.

A METHOD OF
CONTEMPLATIVE PRAYER

There is only one way to become a contemplative, and that is to set aside each day a time and place for prayer that is real, personal, and contemplative. Without the practice of contemplative prayer, no individual and no community can be called contemplative. No amount of other prayers and occupations can make up for this need. Anyone, then, who wishes to become a contemplative must make himself or herself available for contemplative prayer every day.

In addition, whoever strives sincerely to live the contemplation life

- will be involved in a most personal way
- will come face to face with the deepest and truest self
- will be seeking the Spirit of God, who breathes as and when he wills

- will become a pilgrim of the Spirit, always on the move, always more eager to reach the presence of the Lord

Spiritual Preparation

The time spent in silent prayer must be important to aspiring contemplatives in relation to their whole life as religious, as priests, or as laypersons. Most religious experienced their original vocation as a call to a life of surrender to God and of dedication to his service; in addition, God seemed to promise a life in which they would experience, in a personal way, knowledge of him and of his love. This promise is open to all vocations in life.

The intent of contemplative practice is to the fulfillment of this promise. In order to prepare spiritually for this grace, two requirements are necessary.

Movement toward repentance

We must endeavor to express our continued surrender by moving away from violent to nonviolent and peaceful ways; from any kind of false approach to utter truthfulness and inner harmony; from self-love to great sensitivity to the needs, rights, and feelings of others; from self-indulgence to an instinct for purity of heart and mind; from possessiveness and greed to a giving and sharing of all we possess.

In other words, we must resolutely set our face against the vicious tendencies that grieve the Spirit and kill the soul: pride and prestige, jealousy and dislike, anger and violence, self-indulgence and uncleanness, laziness and greed. Conversely, we must welcome with all our heart patience in our manner, kindness toward all, goodness in our intentions, trustfulness in our dealings, gentleness in both our inward and outward bearing, and control of heart and mind.

All this becomes possible to the extent that we open our heart and life to the Spirit of Jesus. Human nature being what it is, therefore, a continual return to repentance is involved.

Desire for union with God

We must continually nourish within ourselves a desire for God and for the fulfillment of the promise he held out from the beginning.

Although we may not have the same intensity of feeling, we should at least understand what the author of the *Cloud* wrote to a friend about this attraction to God:

But when the joyful enthusiasm which seizes you as you read or hear about contemplation is really the touch of God calling you to a higher life of grace, you will notice very different effects. So abounding will it be that it will follow you to bed at night and rise with you in the morning. It will pursue you through the day in everything you do, intruding into your usual daily devotions like a barrier between you and them.

Moreover it will seem to occur simultaneously with that blind desire which, in the meantime, quietly grows in intensity. The enthusiasm and the desire will seem to be part of each other; so much so, that you will think it is only one desire you feel, though you will be at a loss to say just precisely what it is that you long for.

Your whole personality will be transformed, your countenance will radiate an inner beauty, and for as long as you feel it nothing will sadden you. A thousand miles would you run to speak with another who you knew really felt it, and yet when you got there, find yourself speechless. Let others say what they will, your only joy would be to speak of it. Your words will be few, but so fruitful and full of fire that the little you say will hold a world of wisdom (though it may seem nonsense to those still unable to transcend the limits of reason). Your silence will be peaceful, your speech helpful, and your prayer secret in the depths of your being. Your self-esteem will be natural and unspoiled by conceit, your way with others gentle, and your laughter merry, as you take delight in everything with the joy of a child. How dearly you will love to sit apart by yourself, knowing that others, not sharing your desire and attraction, would only hinder you. Gone will be all desire to read or hear books, for your only desire will be to hear of it.

Thus the mounting desire for contemplation and the joyful enthusiasm that seizes you when you read or hear of it meet and become one. These two signs (one interior and one exterior) agree, and you may rely on them as proof that God is calling you to enter within and begin a more intense life of grace.

A similar intense desire for God can be gained from the words of the hymn "Jesu, dulcis memoria":

Jesus to find shall be my care
Deep in my heart, for he is there;
At home, abroad, in storm and fair
My love shall seek him everywhere.

Jesus, my admirable King,
Victor beyond all hallowing,
Sweetness beyond all uttering,
My one desire, my everything.

O blessed, ever-saving fire,
O ever-yearning fond desire,
What more can soul of man require
Than toward thee, Jesus, to aspire!

Come to us, Jesus, Lord and King,
Whose glory choirs of angels sing,
Thy light into our darkness bring,
We wait thee, too long lingering.

Thou satisfaction of the mind,
Thou peace of soul that wanders blind,
My pride, my glory unconfined,
Jesus, the Savior of mankind.

Lead, and I will follow thee, my Guide,
We will not part whate'er betide;
Thou hast my heart within thy side,
Jesus, of man the single pride.

Hymns may hint at, but no words can describe, no book can explain, what it means to love Jesus. We can only know it from personal experience. When he visits our heart, it is bathed in the light of truth. The world loses all its attraction when his love burns within us. Those who have tasted Jesus hunger for more. But only those who love him are able to fulfill their desires—joy now in his embrace and glory later in his kingdom.

Here are two practical ways to feed and strengthen this movement toward repentance and desire for union with God:

Meditative Spiritual Reading. In this kind of reading, we make selections we feel draw us to God and to prayer—selections that, even when taken in small portions, fill our mind and heart with love of and desire for God.

Such reading tends to keep the mind in devout meditation, leading to contemplation. Father Thomas of Jesus, writing about acquired contemplation, says: "Therefore, if you burn with desire for contemplation, apply yourself to devout and continual meditations; it is the infallible way to succeed."

And Dom G. Belorgey writes in *The Practice of Mental Prayer:*

A work impregnated with the divine quality is the only kind a soul should consider. Needless to say, holy Scripture is the first and purest source of all, and a truly recollected reading is both pleasing to God and often instrumental in bringing him back. Now in the state of quietude the soul receives many lights, enabling it to discover new shadings and meanings that were hidden before; these seem to appear effortlessly, and as a kind of enlightening presence is the Holy Spirit. God's gift is a higher, loving knowledge of himself and an increase of faith in his sacred Scriptures.

Desire for the Gift of the Spirit. The gospels make it clear that we must ask with expectant faith for the gift of the Spirit and that our prayer will be heard (Luke 11:13).

The following prayer asks for this gift:

Lord, teach me how to pray, how to know and
    love you in silent prayer.
Lord, pour into me your Spirit in all his fullness.
Lord, let me be possessed by your Spirit,
    so that you may reign in me and through me.
May the Lord be praised. Alleluia!

We should keep in mind the following exhortations as we prepare to enter into contemplative prayer:

- A song of devotion should not be lightly sung.
- Our word should not be lightly given, but once given, it must be kept.
- This prayer should not be lightly started.
- Start only when ready and then never look back.
- The Lord loves us and needs us.
- The Lord is waiting for an opportunity to enter our life.
- Once we begin praying, we will never be the same.
- He will make use of us.
- Contemplative prayer is the greatest gift we will ever receive.

Physical Requisites

After we have prepared ourselves spiritually for contemplative prayer, there are certain physical requisites to be considered.

Where to pray

We should choose a place to pray where we are completely private and alone, where we are unlikely to be disturbed, where there is not too much noise. Jesus says, "When you pray, go to your inner room, close the door, and pray to your Father in secret" (Matthew 6:6). He himself "would withdraw to deserted places to pray" (Luke 5:16). There is comfort in the fact that he did not always succeed (Mark 6:30-33). Being together with others in the same place or room is not advisable, as the very awareness of the presence of others often is a powerful psychological distraction and a hindrance to complete relaxation.

Ideally, the best place is before the Blessed Sacrament, the sacrament of his presence among us. Unfortunately, there is too much distraction and noise in many churches and chapels for silent prayer.

Cardinal Lercaro says the place to pray should be "if possible, in church or in one's room—preferably the latter. If in church, one is likely to be called upon to perform the duties of one's ministry or disturbed for some other reason. Somewhere out of doors would do—but in general, the place to be chosen is that where there is least likelihood of meeting with distractions or interruptions" (*Methods of Mental Prayer*).

How long to pray

If at all possible, at least one full hour daily should be set aside for prayer. This is the traditional time fixed for *mental prayer* in most religious rules. Saint Peter of Alcantara warns that when the time is too short, it is passed in unloading the imagination and in bringing the heart under control. Then, just at the moment when we are ready and ought to be beginning the exercise, we stop it. (It is a sobering thought that one full hour a day represents just about four percent of all the time we live.)

The more active and distracting our daily life, the more need there is of a full hour of "relaxing, coming to rest in God." We need the steadying impact of this *daily* exercise on our nerves and emotions. Those who lead busy lives also need the daily "healing of soul" and "opening to the Spirit" in quiet and silence. In this way, through daily, silent prayer, God changes us and renews us more thoroughly than through other beneficial activities.

In view of all this, the practice of having two separate periods of thirty minutes each instead of one full hour at one time is not advocated. In the beginning, one full hour seems dreadfully long, and during the first weeks or months, perseverance may be an agonizing effort. But gradually, one will get used to this length and attuned to its spirit of quiet leisure spent with and for God.

But make the effort. "So then, take up the toil of the contemplative work with wholehearted and generosity. Beat upon this high 'cloud of unknowing' and spurn the thought of resting. For I tell you frankly that anyone who really desires to be a contemplative will know the pain of arduous toil (unless God should intervene with special grace); he will feel keenly the cost of constant effort until he is long accustomed to this work" (*Cloud*).

(*Editor's note:* Some people, no matter how well-intentioned, may simply be unable to devote one uninterrupted hour a day to prayer due to work or family obligations. Some teachers of prayer recommend beginning with a twenty-minute period of quiet prayer and gradually increasing the time.)

When to pray

When to pray must depend to some extent on what is possible within the framework of our profession and commitments. Some like the early morning: "Rising very early before dawn, he [Jesus] left and went off to a deserted place, where he prayed" (Mark 1:35). The morning quiet may be rewarding to those who are physically and mentally awake. Others prefer the quiet evening before sleep. At this time it is easier to relax and join in "an hour of watch and vigil" with Christ.

In planning prayer time, we can take advantage of otherwise wasted waiting times. Especially after we have become so accustomed to contemplative prayer that it is almost second nature, we can quiet ourselves with the breath and engage in quiet inner prayer while waiting in the doctor's office, the airport, or the bus terminal. These times can be used to supplement regularly scheduled daily prayer times.

Those living in community and bound to mental prayer by

religious rule should perhaps discuss the time problem at a community meeting to determine when each can best engage in this prayer.

It should be noted that this prayer fulfills the obligation of mental prayer or meditation that religious and others have. Does this mean they no longer need to meditate? As a special exercise, meditation may be dropped, but it never actually disappears. Those who seek God in contemplative prayer tend to read and hear the reading from Scripture with greater interest; they reflect on the liturgy and other spiritual reading; they continue to ponder the mysteries and the ways of God.

Posture during prayer

Bodily posture while praying is important, as this has a definite influence on the ability to relax and remain undistracted. The body should be relaxed but attentive; the posture should be comfortable, not a source of strain or tension. Since there is least strain when the back is straight, in a vertical position, hold the back and head as if balancing a book on the head.

Kneeling is the traditional prayer position, but sitting with the back straight may be more relaxing. A low stool, about ten inches high, without a back may be useful. Those accustomed to sitting on the floor will find this position more restful. Again, the back should be held straight.

Many who begin contemplative prayer find it best to keep their eyes open but fixed on some point or object straight ahead. When the eyes wander, the mind follows, and attentiveness is interrupted.

Overcoming Distractions

Wandering thoughts and other distractions often are a problem for contemplatives. Distractions are treated here so those new to contemplative prayer will know how to overcome them even before beginning.

If unable to relax, let tensions go and surrender. If very tired physically and mentally, accept fully this weakness and remember that contemplative prayer is for God and for no advantage of our own. We must be ready to "waste" this part of our time as an immolation poured out for him. In one way, a sense of failure belongs to the essence of prayer because we learn through failure to become truly disinterested. We seek God's presence and love him even when his face is hidden and when his presence is not discerned.

This is true of a more general sense of failure. Imperfections and even sins cry out for humility, which is the necessary condition of prayer. Viewed this way, imperfections and sins seem almost a help rather than a hindrance. To feel utterly crushed and annihilated, incapable of any good, wholly dependent on God's undeserved and infinite mercy—this is the best and only preparation for prayer. Such a state engenders complete confidence and exultation in being nothing because God is all, which brings the only peace that is true peace.

In *Spiritual Letters,* Dom John Chapman advises:

Distractions are two kinds: (a) the ordinary distractions, such as one has in meditation, which take one right away; and (b) the harmless wanderings of the *imagination alone,* while the intellect is (to all appearances) idle and empty, and the will is fixed on God. These are quite harmless.

When these latter distractions remain all the time, the prayer is just as good, often much better. The will remains united; yet we feel utterly dissatisfied and humbled. But we come away *wanting nothing but God.*

Our special concern should be the *harmless wandering* imagination while our heart and will reach out to God and are fixed on him. The two aids that follow should help minimize distractions and keep the awareness focused on God's presence to the greatest possible extent.

Rhythmic breathing

Tension, worry, and excitement all lead to short and shallow breathing. But if we make our breathing more deliberate, slower and more regular (rhythmic), tension ebbs away and we become more relaxed and have a greater sense of peace and serenity.

During contemplative prayer, therefore, we should try to breathe in and out slowly, deeply, and deliberately, to the rhythm of the pulse or heartbeat. More precisely, breathe in through the nose, counting mentally 1, 2, 3, 4, 5, 6, in rhythm with the speed of the heartbeat. Then hold the breath a little (for some counts) and breathe out in the same controlled and slow manner. At the end of the exhalation, pause awhile (for some counts). This rhythmic breathing can be practiced at other times also; for example, when walking or sitting quietly or lying down.

At first, this practice needs conscious attention and control. It will gradually become so habitual, however, that it can be done without thinking.

Father Dominic Hoffman in *The Life Within: The Prayer of Union* gives these helpful hints:

> Although we cannot bring about contemplative prayer by our own volition, there are ways to dispose ourselves for it. These ways each individual will discover for himself. Saint John of the Cross mentions the fact that some places are conducive to prayer rather than others. Likewise there is a technique borrowed from the East, but not unsuited to the West. This is the practice of slow, deep breathing during prayer, tending to hold the breath at the point of exhalation.

Repeated prayers

A suitable prayer that is repeated helps to sustain quiet and rhythmic breathing. The words can be spoken (with the lips or, better, mentally) either while breathing in or breathing out or both. In view of the rhythmic breathing, the prayer should have a certain cadence or rhythm, allowing it to be sustained by the rhythm of the breathing.

The best-known example of this is the Jesus Prayer, also known as the Prayer of the Heart, one form of which is the repetition of the holy name *Jesus, Jesus, Jesus.* Another form of the Jesus Prayer is to repeat *Jesus, Son of the living God, have mercy on me, a sinner.* The prayer is repeated in rhythm with the quiet breathing, while the awareness remains on the Savior.

The Jesus Prayer is described in detail in *The Way of a Pilgrim,* a delightful little spiritual work written by an anonymous Russian peasant in the nineteenth century. Several translations are available. It is also the topic of several publications available from Dove Publications, Pecos, NM 87552. It may be noted that the Jesus Prayer has a scope and application that is far beyond our present concern (an hour of contemplative prayer a day) and is meant to be a never-ceasing prayer of union with God.

Other words may be used for repetition, for example:

Let thy love play upon my voice and rest on my silence.

I, with you on the cross, no longer live; you live in me.

In fact, such prayers can be formulated specifically to express the phase of prayer we are in, provided that the prayer really expresses what we want to say and that its language is rhythmic, even if the rhythm is not perfect. We might formulate a prayer of surrender, acceptance, love, praise, thanksgiving, and so on.

We may choose to repeat part of the Lord's Prayer in the same manner. Either say a very short prayer like *Abba, Father* or extend it to *Abba, Father, glorify your name* or make a longer prayer of the whole first part sustained on a long quiet outgoing breath: *Our Father in heaven, holy be your name, your kingdom come, your will be done on earth as in heaven.* Such prayer may be a powerful intercession for his kingdom in ourselves and others "for the glory of his name."

Finally, when physically or mentally too weary to pray otherwise, we can use the rosary prayer, quietly telling the beads, pacing the Hail Marys gently and rhythmically in harmony with the breathing and dwelling with love on one of the mysteries of faith. Ten to fifteen such decades can be prayed in an hour.

It is helpful to use the rosary beads also for the other repeated prayers during this hour of quiet prayer.

During the first few months after I had begun this hour of prayer, I used to keep my eyes open to avoid distractions and fixed on an object such as a crucifix or the tabernacle or on a fixed point. I did not even look at my watch because when my eyes shift, the focus of my attention on God is also interrupted.

After some months I was satisfied with keeping my eyes closed throughout the prayer time. To have a sense of the passage of time, I use the rosary beads, slipping the beads through my fingers on the rhythm of my breathing. Four times round a rosary and I am close to the end of the hour. At this point I may check the time on my watch.

Twelve Phases of Contemplation

Having made the above preparations, we are now ready to enter into contemplative prayer. In the course of contemplation, we can go through or dwell in twelve different phases. Depending on actual circumstances or personal needs, we can dwell in or stay in one phase rather than another. Or we can restrict ourselves to just one phase.

For the first few days, it may be good to spend the hour

quietly seeking and remaining in an awareness of the Lord's presence and then, by way of exercise, go through the phases, taking one a day. After this we should be guided each day by our needs. From the start we should keep in mind that "how we live" will determine the quality of our contemplation.

AN OVERVIEW OF
THE TWELVE PHASES OF PRAYER

Phases 1-3: *Relaxation and Silence, Awareness of God's Presence, Longing Love*

In these phases, we seek God and reach out to him.

Phases 4-7: *Surrender, Acceptance, Forgiving from the Heart, Repentance and Forgiveness*

These are concerned with purification of heart and mind, which must become free and transparent to him.

Phases 8-11: *Asking in Faith, Contemplation, Receiving, Intercession*

These are concerned with receiving (from) God and loving him. "All these things will be given you..." (Matthew 6:33).

Phase 12: *Praise and Thanksgiving*

This phase is the end of contemplative prayer.

1. Relaxation and silence

Sit down and relax, slowly and deliberately letting all tension flow away.

Gently seek an awareness of the immediate and personal presence of God. There is no violence in this movement, no suppression of moods, feelings, frustrations. Suppression implies violence and increases tension. Just relax and let go of everything as you enter into the awareness of God's presence.

We can relax and let go of everything precisely *because* God is present. In his presence nothing really matters; all things are in his hands. Tension, anxiety, worry, frustration, all melt away before him as snow before the sun.

Seek peace and inner silence. Let the mind, heart, will, and emotions become tranquil and serene. Allow inner storms to subside: obsessional thoughts, passionate drives of will and emotions. "Seek peace and pursue it" (Psalm 34:15).

Be ready, if necessary, to spend all the prayer time like this without any thought of result or effect or reward, to be ready thus to "waste" time, to make it a naked, selfless offering of time and attention for God alone.

This movement toward peace and silence elicits an inflow of grace; it creates conditions for a genuine, true, and personal love for God to be awakened in the spirit.

Moreover, this movement is not just a neutral, psychological event. It is a movement of surrender and acceptance of God's will that enables the heart, will, and emotions to become impregnated with God's gift of peace and his will to nonviolent love.

Some may feel that relaxation, coupled with quiet breathing, tends to make them fall asleep. Here, however, we seek to become relaxed in order to be awake and alert to the presence of God, rather like a sentry who makes himself quiet in order to listen for the presence of others. The mind, nerves, and emotions are stilled so the heart may be ready to contemplate.

2. Awareness of God's presence

Open yourself entirely to an awareness of God's presence.

He is present to our spirit, attentive to our awareness. He dwells at the center of our true self, at the core of our being. Now we *seek* an awareness of this, but one day he will *give* us this awareness freely.

He is closer to our true self than we are ourselves. He knows us better than we know ourselves. He loves us better than we love ourselves. He is "Abba, Father," to us. WE ARE because HE IS.

In the mirror of created existence, we are his living image and likeness. When we know, we reflect his knowledge. When we love, we reflect his love. When we call out to him, he hears. When we seek his awareness, he awakens us to his presence in and through Jesus. He speaks his word of love: "You are my son, you are my daughter, beloved of me, in whom I am well pleased."

In and through and with Jesus, he pours out his Spirit, making us call out "Abba, Father." He fills us with thanks and praise for his wonderful presence.

3. Longing love

"By love he can be caught and held, but by thinking never" (*Cloud,* Chapter 6). Love for someone who is as yet absent is expressed in longing, in love and desire, in a longing love. Love for someone who is present is expressed in communication: receiving his loving presence, giving love from our heart, expressing love in words, in touching, in self-giving.

Begin with an awareness of the emptiness of your heart. Then, in silence, seek him with longing, reaching out to him.

The picture is that of a person who in complete darkness reaches out to his loved one who is somewhere in the present, nearby, within reach.

It is the heart that reaches out (hands tend to express what is in the heart); it is not the mind that can touch him. The mind thinks and reflects about an absent person. As soon as the person enters, the mind stops thinking about him or her. Instead, there is a communication of presence: a giving and taking in of the reality of one another. "He may well be loved, but not thought" (*Cloud,* Chapter 6).

We can express our "longing love" in two ways that go together.

a) **By a slow, deep, rhythmic breathing.** As we breathe in, we want to breathe in his loving presence; after holding the breath for one or two seconds, we breathe out slowly but fully all that is not him. We can spend all our time in this way.

b) **By invoking the holy Name.** We call on him repeatedly with the rhythm of our breathing, repeating the name of *Jesus* or of *Abba, our Father* three times while breathing in and three times while breathing out.

This is not a mechanical repetition of sounds like the mantra in Eastern meditation methods but a loving invocation of the heart. All the while, we keep the attention of mind and heart as much as possible on God.

Only *Jesus* should be invoked or *Abba, our Father.* We have been baptized in their name and in no other.

When we begin this Jesus Prayer or Father Prayer, several things might happen. Initially, we repeat the sounds with our lips (vocal prayer). After some time, we begin repeating the words mentally while the lips remain silent (mental prayer). Gradually, we begin repeating the name in our heart. When this happens, our heart has awakened and has begun to pray. As an ancient Eastern Christian tradition has it, the prayer has "descended from the head into the heart." Once the heart has begun to pray, there is an inflow of grace by which we know God in our heart.

4. Surrender

Spending time surrendering ourselves to God is fulfilling his commandment: "You shall love the Lord, your God, with all your heart, with all your soul, and with all your mind" (Matthew 22:37). Our way of loving him lies in surrendering every part of our being to him and seeking to be loved and filled by him. The Sabbath was instituted to give us adequate time to give him our attention, love, and surrender.

Before God's face, aware of his presence, surrender every aspect of your being: your hands and wrists and arms, your head and ears and senses and brain, your feet and legs, every nerve and muscle and blood vessel and organ.

We return ourselves to him. We seek to withdraw our possessiveness and beg him to possess us, to live in and through us, so that the life we live is not our own but Christ living in us. (See Galatians 2:20.) We ask him to accept all as an instrument of peace and render it a clean obligation.

Surrender your cares and worries.

We grow in an awareness that there is no ground for anxiety and tension if our faith and hope in him are true. He takes care of and looks after his sons and daughters. So we let go of everything that preoccupies us in a movement of faith and surrender. From now on we let him lead us, step by step.

Surrender your heart, your feelings, your love.

Our heart does not love with its own love. "Everyone who loves is begotten by God and knows God" (1 John 4:7). It is Jesus, who through his Spirit, loves his Father in "our" breath of love. It is not we who love but he loves in us, through us. And his love is quiet, serene, ineffable, and enduring.

Surrender your whole personality, feelings and all.

We feel our way toward a gentle love and beyond our thinking "to where he waited near—whose presence well I knew—in a place where no one else appeared" (Saint John of the Cross, *Poems*).

Our fervent prayer is that in this silence he may pour out his Spirit and begin to live and reign in us.

Surrender yourself to Jesus, your Savior, and accept him as your Lord. He has prayed and suffered to free us and claim us as his own. Say to him: "Take me and all I have, and do with me whatever you will. Send me where you will. Use me as you will. I surrender myself and all I possess absolutely and entirely, unconditionally and forever, to your control."

This phase can grow into ardent and insistent supplication for the outpouring and the gifts of the Holy Spirit, for an overwhelming sense of his presence and peace. And the supplication always ends in faith that he has already heard your prayer (Mark 11:24).

5. Acceptance

Many of our "natural" reactions are expressions and gestures of nonacceptance, of rebellion, of running away from reality, of suppression. Our anger flares up, impatience possesses us like an evil spirit, dislikes and grudges harden our heart. We resent interference and interruption. Without always realizing it, we refuse to accept persons, events, situations, conditions—even ourselves as God wills them for us and as he accepts them for us.

Nonacceptance of God's will in concrete circumstances is experienced in prayer as a barrier, a roadblock on our way to God. It is his will that we accept people, circumstances, events, as they actually are and occur; that we never try to influence people or events by means of violence of the heart; that we bring them only the power of love and forgiveness, of suffering, acceptance, and thanksgiving. In daily life this means that we should never judge, never argue, never criticize, never be violent, and always try to mind our own business.

Become aware of persons and situations in your life where there is a barrier of nonacceptance.

Look at each barrier and deliberately accept God's will in regard to it. Withdraw self-oriented and condemnatory judgment and criticism. Try to develop an attitude of genuine regret for violence in thought, word, and deed, risking a leap of faith and love.

When we turn our heart toward God, he makes "all things work for good for those who love God, who are called according to his purpose" (Romans 8:28).

Acceptance of his will is identical with acceptance of his guidance, his lordship, as he leads us step by step through the concrete circumstances of our daily life. He guides us and leads us into his kingdom through his will for us. His kingdom comes to us where we accept and do his will.

Lay down your own will and try to discern God's will.

Our own thoughts and plans lose their compulsion as we seek to see his plan as it unfolds and as we try to follow his pattern.

6. Forgiving from the heart

The God we seek is love, full of compassion and forgiveness. Even before we repent and seek his mercy, his forgiveness is ready and waiting for us. He calls us to be like him, our heavenly Father, as true sons and daughters (Matthew 5:44-45, 48). Jesus, his beloved Son, has manifested his true Sonship also in unreserved love and forgiveness toward those who hurt him: "Father, forgive them, they know not what they do" (Luke 23:34).

Few things close our hearts to God's grace and to his loving presence as much as resentment, unforgiveness, and hurt feelings. Our hearts were created for loving and for being channels of his love from deep within our being. But resentment and unforgiveness block and poison our hearts. As the psalmist sang, "Do not harden your hearts..." (Psalm 95:8).

The first step is the decision to forgive the one who has hurt us, a decision made by an act of the will. But more is needed. Our hearts need to be cleansed of bitterness and healed of hurt and pain so we can remember what has happened with undisturbed inner peace.

Close your eyes as you sit before the Lord and recall the memory for which you seek the healing of forgiveness. Reenter the situation by visualizing the place and person(s) involved. Imagine Jesus himself coming to you there.

Actually, he *was* with you, but you did not notice him at the time. What would he do for you? He would surely love you and ask you to forgive the other person. So address that person directly, repeating the words "In Jesus' name, I forgive you from my heart."

Continue to pray like this until you can "see" the Lord loving that person and are able to love and accept the person also. This is the best way to come to this deeper cleansing and healing.

When there is a deep hurt, all the prayer time may be needed to work on this one memory-relationship. Indeed, it is worth giving it all the time. At another time you may want to make a list of three to eight persons you dislike. Then, beginning with the first, pray as above for each one on the list. This will open the inner heart to the grace of contemplative prayer.

7. Repentance and forgiveness

When we enter this phase, we may be oppressed by sense of sin and failure. It may be a general sense of sin and unworthiness, or it may be due to a sorry state we fell into only now. We must face this barrier in a spirit of genuine repentance and true humility.

Confess your sins and failings and beg God's forgiveness, thanking him most humbly for hearing your prayer.

Then face him as you are: sinful, spiritually handicapped, and disabled in many ways, a chronic patient. Accept these handicaps and disabilities because God accepts you and loves you as you are.

This moment is no time to nurse a sense of guilt. Accept and embrace God's forgiveness and love fully and completely. Guilt and inferiority feelings before him are expressions of selfishness or self-centeredness. In indulging them, we give greater importance to our little sinful self than to his immense and never-ending love.

Surrender to God your guilt and inferiority.

Accept his joy in loving and forgiving you. Spend some quiet time letting all this sink into your consciousness. It is a healing grace to surrender our sinfulness to God's mercy.

When we are unable to pray for no precise reason except a sense of uneasy and unworthiness, this quotation from the *Cloud* may help:

Now we know that all evil, either by instigation or deed, is summed up in the one word "sin." So when we ardently desire to pray for the destruction of evil let us say and think and mean nothing else but this little word "sin" (Chapter 39).

Immerse your being in the spiritual reality signified by the word *sin* without dwelling on any particular kind of sin, such as pride, anger, envy, greed, sloth, gluttony, or lust, or on whether it is mortal or venial sin.

What does the kind or gravity of the sin matter? Anything that separates a contemplative from God, however slightly, appears as a grievous evil and robs him or her of inner peace.

Let yourself experience sin as a *lump,* realizing that it is yourself, but without defining it precisely. Then cry out in your heart this one word "sin," "sin," "sin," or "help," "help," "help." God can teach you what I mean through experience far better than I can with words. For it is best when this word is wholly interior without a definite thought or actual sound. Yet occasionally, you will be satiated with the meaning of sin that the sorrow and burden of it will flow over your body and soul and you may burst out with the word itself (*Cloud,* Chapter 40).

Repeatedly pray "Lord, have mercy!" or "Jesus, forgive me my sins!" until he gives the grace of compunction and melts the lump of sin within you.

8. Asking in faith

Prayer is not something we do on our own. When we take one step toward God, he moves toward us. Two steps hasten his coming in grace.

First, **accept, at a definite time and place, Jesus as your**

personal Lord and Savior. This means accepting him and yielding to him at a deep and personal level. To do this, you might say the following prayer:

> All my prayer is that in this silence he may pour out his Spirit and begin to live and reign in me....I surrender myself to Jesus, my Savior, and accept him as my Lord.

He always responds to this acceptance, which enables him to manifest his lordship and saving power to you. This act of acceptance may seem deceptively simple and perhaps superfluous, but the results are surprising. Mary took the first step, accepting God as her own Lord, becoming his servant, and singing his praises.

Next, **pray to be baptized in the Holy Spirit.** The following prayer begins to release into our conscious awareness the graces of the Holy Spirit dwelling in us through the sacraments:

> Come, Holy Spirit, fill my heart, now surrendered to Jesus, my Savior, my Lord. Enkindle in me the fire of divine Love. Fill me with the glorious presence of my risen Lord so that I may no longer live but he lives in me.

For many, this step opens the way to *infused* contemplative prayer. For others, it is strengthened and renewed. In this new life in the Spirit, knowledge and love of God becomes a personally experienced reality, meant to lead to a radical insertion into the mystery of the Body of Christ.

This phase can grow into an ardent and insistent supplication for the Holy Spirit: for the outpouring of the Spirit, for the gifts of the Spirit, for an overwhelming sense of the peace and presence of the Spirit in the core of our being.

9. Contemplation

By now we have put away all obstacles in our heart, all thinking in our mind, all wavering in our will: "God alone I seek and desire, only him" (*Cloud,* Chapter 7).

Be content to feel this mysterious grace sweetly awaken in the depths of your spirit. Forget everything but God and fix on him your naked desire, your longing stripped of all self-interest" (*Cloud,* Chapter 34).

Lift your heart up to the Lord with a gentle stirring of love desiring him for his own sake and not for his gifts. Center all your attention and desire on him and let this be the sole concern of your mind and heart (*Cloud,* Chapter 3).

Think only of God, the God who created you, redeemed you, and guided you to this work. Allow no other ideas about God to enter your mind. Yet even this is too much. A naked intent toward God, the desire for him alone, is enough" (*Cloud,* Chapter 7).

Turn yourself entirely to his presence. Steadily look at him. His presence becomes more real to us. He holds our inward sight. Our glance simply and lovingly rests on him.

Our prayer is nothing but a loving awareness of him: "I look because I love; I look in order to love, and my love is fed and influenced by looking..." (Domitry V. Lehodey, *The Ways of Mental Prayer*).

Be quiet and exist in a calm and simple awareness of God's presence. Let your heart seek him out and open to receive his love. It is wordless prayer, fed by a quiet ardor. There is a darkness that thought and clear knowledge cannot bridge, but only longing love: "Let your longing relentlessly beat upon the *cloud of unknowing* that lies between you and your God. Pierce that cloud with the keen shaft of your love..." (*Cloud,* Chapter 12).

Saint John of the Cross, in this excerpt from his poem *The Dark Night,* describes how he reaches out to God in love:

Upon that lucky night
in secrecy, inscrutable to sight,
I went without discerning
and with no other light
except for that which in my heart was burning.

It lit and led me through
more certain than the light of noonday clear
to where he waited near
—whose presence well I knew—
in a place where no one else appeared.

This phase may well be sustained by a repeated prayer, intensified by quiet rhythmic breathing.

10. Receiving

God always responds. He cannot refuse a seeking in faith and love. "Seek and you will always find" becomes "Seek and you will always be found." He seeks us before we seek him, while we seek him, and after we have sought him, "The LORD appears to him from afar: With age-old love I have loved you; so I have kept my mercy toward you" (Jeremiah 31:3).

He responds. He turns to us. He seeks us. He is anxious to invade our spirit. He wants his Spirit to possess us.

Bask in the warmth of his love. Feel his gaze upon you.

Jesus, our Lord, is eager to possess our heart with which to love his Father and with which to radiate his love.

Jesus says: "Whoever loves me will keep my word, and my Father will love him, and we will come to him and make our dwelling with him" (John 14:23).

"We have come to know and to believe in the love God has for us. God is love, and whoever remains in love remains in God and God in him" (1 John 4:16-17).

He fills us with his presence, with his Spirit. We may discern him only in faith or, through his grace, in experience.

His presence brings a deep spiritual peace, a share in his Sabbath rest, a greater serenity, an ability to accept and to suffer, a lifting of despair, a welling up of joy and love, a flood of grace, a strong desire to praise and thank him.

Or if such be his will, it brings power to serve him and proclaim him, to bear witness to his kingdom, to bring healing to his name, to bring peace and unity to people of goodwill.

11. Intercession

There is need for intercession. Jesus continues to save us through his uninterrupted intercession (Hebrews 7:25). In some way he also needs to use our heart for this intercession. True, we seek the Giver rather than the gift, but the Giver seeks to save his people. Through his Spirit in us, he is concerned for all those who should be his people; in us he wants to intercede and suffer.

We must pray and never become weary, with simple and expectant faith (Luke 18:1). His promise is there: "Ask and you will always receive." We must learn to pray with faith that he has already given what we ask for, as the Lord has urged us to pray. "All that you ask for in prayer, believe that you will receive it and it shall be yours" (Mark 11:24).

Pray according to his will for his kingdom in ourselves and in others (1 John 5:14-15).

Often we may wish to intercede in the following way at the end of prayer.

Lord, teach me how to pray. Glorify your name. Your kingdom come; your will be done in my life and the lives of others. Grant your peace to _____. Help _____ in his or her need. Lord, make your love known to _____.

12. Praise and thanksgiving

Jesus invariably thanked and praised his Father and taught his disciples to do the same. The priestly prayer of Jesus (John 17) is one of praise, thanksgiving, and intercession.

When he has made known his presence, touched you with his Spirit, or filled you with his grace and peace, begin spontaneously to thank and praise him.

Ideally, the time will come when we begin to thank him as we share in the loneliness and suffering of Jesus, simply because his will is being done in us.

SCHEDULE FOR A
SELF-DIRECTED EIGHT-DAY
CONTEMPLATIVE RETREAT

If at all possible, spend a full hour every day in this silent prayer. If you feel drawn to it and have the time, you might wish to take an hour twice a day, morning and evening, during this eight-day retreat period.

Find a place that invites you to prayer. It may be a chapel, a spot in the garden, or simply your own room. Whatever place you choose, it should be somewhere you can sit undisturbed, with your back straight.

First Day: Seek Him With All Your Heart

1. Relax and become silent.

Begin breathing deeply and slowly, giving attention to your own physical reality. Then close your eyes and listen to all the sounds that you can hear, near and far. Try to identify each sound. Finally, turn your attention to your self, your spiritual heart, the center of your being. Spend five to ten minutes in silent, attentive relaxation.

2. Make an Act of Faith.

Try to experience the real and living presence of God within you. Next, try to relate to him in a personal way. A good method is through a dialogue of speaking and listening. The imagination is a powerful faculty for actualizing faith. Spend ten minutes or so on this step.

3. Make an Act of Contrition.

Allow your sins and failings to come to mind. God is holy. Confess each sin to him, asking his pardon and receiving it with a humble and grateful heart. Spend about ten minutes on this step.

4. Make an Act of Hope.

Open your heart in hope and expectation. I know a woman who, on rising each morning, prepares for her hour of prayer with the thought *I'm going to meet the Lord.* If you do not expect any grace from him in this hour, he may not be able to give you anything. Some approach this daily hour of prayer as a routine, going through the motions as if sitting down at the table, saying grace, and rising to leave—and all the while there is no food on the table! And they think this is normal! No, open your heart in expectation. He has prepared a banquet for you. Take ten minutes to reflect in hopeful expectation.

5. Make an Act of Love.

Reach out to God with love and desire: "By love he may be caught and held, but by thinking never" (*Cloud,* Chapter 6).

Allow the deepest longing of your heart to come to the surface. In faith, seek him for all that you need. (Use the rest of the hour for this step.)

Second Day: Seek Him, Invoking His Name

After you have seated yourself, relax and become attentive as directed on the first day. Then go through yesterday's Acts of Faith, Contrition, Hope, and Love.

Next, begin to express your longing love through your breathing with the invocation of his name as described in Phase 3, "Longing Love" (page 58).

First, focus your attention on your spiritual heart, where he is present. Then, begin repeating his name, trying to keep your attention (a) on his name and (b) in your heart. Whenever your mind wanders, gently lead it back to the holy name.

Third Day: Surrender

As you begin to focus your attention on God and become aware of his presence, surrender your whole being and every part of your being—physical, mental, emotional, and spiritual—into his hands. Do this deliberately, consciously, and verbally.

The Lord does not ask you to renounce what you are or what you have. Rather, he asks that you *entrust* all you have and are into his hands and into his loving care and that you live in total trust and in pure faith in him. Surrendering is your way of loving him and accepting his love. Hearts and lives that are surrendered become channels of his love, peace, and presence. (Refer to Phase 4, "Surrender," pages 59 to 61.)

Fourth Day: Accept

As you begin to turn your attention to him and reach out to him, deliberately allow negative feelings and dislikes to come to mind, especially people and situations that irritate and annoy you, things you tend to criticize and grumble about, such as ill health, the weather, food, other people's habits, and society in general.

"Every event is adorable—Everything is in God's hands, for those who love him. He accepts every event and loves me through everything that happens. I repent of my own inner violence and come to a deep acceptance of his concrete will for me in every circumstance. Through my faith-acceptance, he can make me an instrument of change for the better where needed and where possible." (Refer to Phase 5, "Acceptance," pages 61 to 62.)

Fifth Day: Forgive and Repent

On this day I suggest two separate hours on themes which, though distinct, cannot be separated.

1. Forgive Everyone From the Heart
After entering into prayer, seek purification and healing of your heart as in Phase 6, "Forgiving From the Heart," pages 62 to 63.

2. Repent and Receive Forgiveness

Similarly, seek purification and healing of heart through recalling your sins, confessing them to the Lord, and receiving his forgiveness in faith as in Phase 7, "Repentance and Forgiveness," pages 64 to 65.

In his holy Presence, ask him to reveal your sins and failings to you. Then confess and seek his mercy. Our sorrow is that our sins have kept our hearts away from him and have made us blind:

Amazing grace! How sweet the sound
That saved a wretch like me!
I once was lost, but now am found,
was blind, but now I see.

Sixth Day: Ask in Faith

In this hour seek his Presence in your heart through the working of the Holy Spirit. Come to Jesus in personal faith, and in his name ask for your heart to be filled, as in Phase 8, "Asking in Faith," pages 65 to 67. Will not your heavenly Father give his holy Spirit when you ask him? (Luke 11:13)

"All life, all holiness comes from you through your Son, Jesus Christ our Lord, by the working of the Holy Spirit" (Third Eucharistic Prayer).

Seventh Day: Practice Contemplation

Receive God's presence and become aware of him in your heart. (Refer to Phase 9, "Contemplation," pages 67 to 68.) As you grow in the grace of this phase, you will begin to recognize his presence in your heart. It will gradually fill your whole being as you become more and more transparent to his presence.

He dwells in me (in my heart) and I dwell in him (in his heart). In this way I become one with him, while remaining distinct. My one desire is to be in his perfect will, and to do it every moment.

Eighth Day: Hold Him and Never Let Him Go

In this hour of prayer, turn your attention to God within you as usual. Let the repeating of his name be a constant expression of your love. Give love and receive love. Give praise and thanksgiving. Ask him to speak to your heart and listen to what he is saying to you this hour—and then respond to his words.

On this last day, you decide to "hold" him and never let him go. In practice, this means a personal decision to give him an hour of your time each and every day.

This hour I give to him whatever it may cost me;
This giving of my time is an offering of love to him,
    expressing the devotion in my heart;
I will give him this hour daily
    in times of joy and sorrow,
        of consolation and dryness;
This hour is for him alone,
    and not for what I will get out of it;
It expresses my self-gift to him who is my everything.

SUGGESTED READING

The Collected Works of St. John of the Cross, trans. Kieran Kavanaugh and Otilio Rodriguez. Washington, D.C.: ICS Publications, 1991.

Haughey, John C. *Conspiracy of God: The Holy Spirit in Men.* New York: Doubleday, 1973.

Johnson, William. *Being in Love: The Practice of Christian Prayer.* San Francisco: HarperSan Francisco, 1992.

Johnston, William, intro. *The Cloud of Unknowing* and *The Book of Privy Counseling.* New York: Doubleday, 1973.

Keating, Thomas. *Open Mind, Open Heart: The Contemplative Dimension of the Gospel.* Rockport, MA: Element Books, 1991.

_____. *Invitation to Love: The Way of Christian Contemplation.* Rockport, MA: Element Books, 1992.

Merton, Thomas. *Contemplative Prayer.* New York: Doubleday, 1971.

St. Teresa of Avila. *Interior Castle.* New York: Doubleday, 1972.

_____. *Way of Perfection.* New York: Doubleday, 1991.

These books are not available from Liguori Publications. Order from your local bookstore.

Other helpful books from Liguori Publications...

You *Can* Know God
by Marilyn Gustin

In this book, Gustin turns to the writings of 14 Christian mystics to show you how you can experience God right where you are—in your home, at work, with family, and with friends. You truly *can* know God. *$9.95*

St. John of the Cross
A Retreat With Father Ernest Larkin, O.Carm.

Treat yourself to a home retreat with this audio set based on the writings and poetry of Saint John of the Cross. Listeners will learn how the journey to the inner renewal and union with God relates to contemporary spirituality. *$29.95*

From Triumph Books...

Thomas Merton
Contemplative Critic
by Henri J.M. Nouwen

A unique meditation on the life and writings of renowned monk, Thomas Merton, this book encourages our own exploration of and expansion in the ways of silence and prayerful solitude. *$7.95*

Ascent of Mount Carmel
by Saint John of the Cross

This one-volume edition of this spiritual classic offers keen insight into human psychology as Saint John guides readers through the step-by-step progress a soul makes in the life of the spirit. *$9.95*

Living Flame of Love
by Saint John of the Cross

In this classic of spirituality, Saint John of the Cross interprets the highest aspirations and emotions of the human soul and eloquently tells of a love more completely refined—and of a soul which has experienced close union with God. *$7.95*

Order from your local bookstore or write to
Liguori Publications
Box 060, Liguori, MO 63057-9999
(Please add $1 for postage and handling for
orders under $5; $1.50 for orders between $5 and $15;
$2 for orders over $15.)
For faster service call toll-free (800) 325-9521, ext. 060.
Please have Visa or MasterCard ready.